D1571603

COACHING ZONE OFFENSES

ATTACKING UNCONVENTIONAL DEFENSES

Bob Huggins

ISBN: 1-58518-174-9

Library of Congress Catalog Card Number: 99-69029
Cover Design: Charles L. Peters
Interior Design: Janet Wahlfeldt
Editor: David Hamburg

Coaches Choice Books is a division of: Coaches Choice
                                           P.O. Box 1828
                                           Monterey, CA 93942
                                           Web Site: http://www.coacheschoiceweb.com

CONTENTS

PREFACE

This book is one of a multivolume series that I have written for Coaches Choice. The series is designed to cover a variety of offensive and defensive concepts that I have used successfully over the years in coaching basketball. Each book is intended for coaches and aspiring coaches at all competitive levels. These ideas have worked for us at the college level, but also for my father, who was a successful high school coach for many years.

Each of the volumes in the series is based not only on my experience as a player and coach, but also on the study of other publications and videos, talking with other coaches, and attending many basketball clinics. To all those people who have shared their time and expertise with me, I want to express my gratitude.

INTRODUCTION

Teams that do not have fundamentally sound offenses that are designed to attack zone defenses will find themselves consistently having to play against zones. Coaches must have an understanding of offensive principles and concepts that are effective against zones and can be incorporated into their offensive system. The more you as a coach understand about a variety of zone attacks, the more you can also adjust your offense to fit the personnel you have each year. A zone offense that has been designed specifically for your players and that they completely understand is an offense that they will believe in.

Just like zone defenses, zone offenses come in all shapes and sizes. Each different zone defense comes with its own strengths and weaknesses. It becomes part of the coach's responsibility to be able to quickly identify the zone and to know how to attack it successfully. In this book, we will attempt to cover what constitutes a good zone offense—and why. Our hope is that we can make you think about what we do conceptually and how you can use some of the ideas in your own zone offensive philosophy. If nothing else, we hope this book makes you think. Too many times as coaches we carry on the same ideas year after year without ever thinking of how to change or improve upon them. I encourage you to constantly challenge yourself and your staff to look at new offensive and defensive concepts.

This book will cover the following areas:

- Overview of how to beat zones

- Player job descriptions and placement of personnel

- Terminology

- Techniques

- Entries into half-court zone offenses

- Zone offensive sets

= player with the ball

COACH = **C**

OFFENSIVE PLAYER = ◯

SPECIFIC OFFENSIVE PLAYERS = ① ② ③ ④ ⑤

OFFENSIVE PLAYER WITH THE BALL = ♂

DEFENSIVE PLAYER = X

SPECIFIC DEFENSIVE PLAYERS = X_1 X_2 X_3 X_4 X_5

PASS = - - - ▶

CUT OR PATH OF THE PLAYER = ⟶

DRIBBLER = ∿∿∿

SCREEN = ⟶|

OFFENSIVE PLAYER 04 WHO STARTS WITH THE BALL, PASSES IT TO 02 AND THEN SCREENS FOR 03, WHO USES HIS SCREEN TO CUT

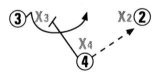

CHAPTER 1

Overview on How to Beat Zones

A few basic basketball principles must be understood when developing any zone offense. Part of the responsibility of the coach is to know as much as possible about the defense he is planning to attack. In order to be a good zone offensive coach, you must have some knowledge of zones from the defensive perspective.

We need to examine exactly what we are attempting to do with our zone offense. Scoring can be accomplished in a variety of methods. Certainly, the simplest way to score is to have good shooters and then get good shots. One essential component of any team offense is identifying what is a good shot for each different player and then continually moving players to the positions on the floor where they can be the most successful and keep the defense honest. Much of this is accomplished through the concepts of overloading and distorting the zone.

The second component after getting a good first shot is to get as many as it takes to score. Therefore, offensive rebounding is a huge key to our success. It then becomes obvious that we must develop an offense that provides opportunities for our best rebounders to get to the boards. There have been seasons where it was said that our best offense was a missed shot. Under the job description of our high post player, you will see that one responsibility listed is to crash the weakside boards on every shot taken. Research tells us that 74 percent of all missed shots go long. It makes sense to play to those odds.

Penetration is the third component of fundamental zone offense. Penetration is one of the methods we use to produce two-on-one situations which break down zones and provide passing angles necessary for easy shots.

The final component for success against zones is ball movement. Reversing the ball from one side of the zone to the other and back, as well as from the interior to the perimeter of the offense, makes the individual defenders in the zone continue to adjust and cover more territory.

In summary, the objectives of our zone offensive principles are as follows:

- To provide shooting opportunities for our good shooters by utilizing intelligent player movement and by distorting the zone

- To enable our best rebounders to get to the correct position on the offensive boards and then rebound with a vengeance

- To use dribble penetration to create two-on-one situations

- To make the zone shift by employing purposeful ball movement

All zones are based on the same principle of defending an area and the ball instead of a player and the ball. Good zone offenses can exploit this principle by understanding the exact territory that each defender is responsible for and therefore where the gaps exist for cutting, dribble penetration, passing and rebounding.

CHAPTER 2

Individual Positions and Job Descriptions

INDIVIDUAL POSITION SKILLS AND JOB DESCRIPTIONS

The following pages will tell you how to decide where you can place your players to give them the best chance to be successful. The job descriptions will help your players to understand the expectations for the position they are playing and also alert them to which areas of their game they will need to work on to be successful according to their particular job description.

POINT GUARD:

- Our best ball handler

- Our best decision maker

- Unselfish mentally

- Quarterback of the club; knows everyone's responsibilities

- Plays mainly in the shaded area shown in Diagram 1

- Shoots well enough to keep perimeter defenders honest

- Able to create two-on-one situations with penetration

- Best perimeter passer; responsible for ball movement

- Throws the lob pass effectively

- Responsible for defensive balance; our best transition defender

WINGS:

- Generally our best spot-up shooters

- Second and third best perimeter passers

- Understand how and when to move without the ball

- Find, penetrate and exploit gaps in the zone to create two-on-one situations

- Can crash the boards from the perimeter to get the offensive rebound

- Good post feeders

- Each one may occasionally be the third man in the post area, so he should understand post principles and have some post-up skills

- Most responsible for player movement

- Whichever wing is the 2 guard has the responsibility for controlling the ball in defensive transition

- Normally plays in the shaded area shown in Diagram 2

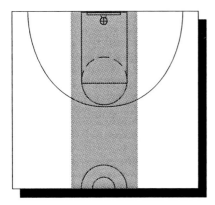

Diagram 1

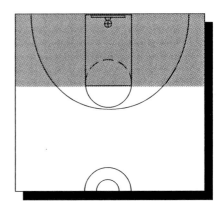

Diagram 2

POSTS:

- Our best post-up players

- Able to perform in both the high post and the low post

- Our best offensive rebounders—*must rebound on the weak side*

- Good post-to-post passers

- Good passers out of the post (especially from the high post)

- Understand and perform the four looks out of the high post (described in the "high post reversal" section of the book)

- Can shoot the short corner shot

- Good footwork that enables them to get and hold the post position and pivot in traffic once they have caught the ball

- High-percentage foul shooters, because they will be on the line often

- Able to keep a body on people at all times to occupy the defense and exaggerate the area they are attempting to cover

- Play in the shaded area shown in Diagram 3

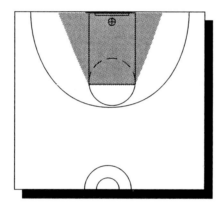

Diagram 3

CHAPTER 3

Zone Offense Terminology

In this chapter, we will introduce to you the terms we use to teach zone offense. Every team has its own terminology. It is only important that the staff and the players on your team understand the language and are consistent in its use.

TERM: OVERLOAD

An *overload* is simply an alignment in which the offensive team has placed more players on one section of the court than there are defenders to guard them. This alignment needs to be accomplished with correct spacing so that one defender cannot guard two offensive players easily. At the college level, we generally consider 15 to 17 feet apart to be adequate spacing between players. Your spacing will depend on the age, quickness and strength of your players. We will describe two different types of team overloads—a triangle and a box:

1. *The Triangle Overload* (Diagram 4). The diagram provides an example of a triangle overload. Even though it calls for the same number of defenders as offensive players, O4 sets up below or under the defensive guard, X1, so as to force X4 to decide whether he should stay with the low post or move up and cover the high post area. O3 has the ball and the responsibility of spacing himself so that he occupies defender X3.

Diagram 4

2. *The Box Overload* (Diagram 5). The diagram shows a box overload. The offense has created a situation with correct spacing and more offensive players than defenders to put the defense at a disadvantage. If X1 and X3 stay matched up with players in their area, then X4 has to decide whether to leave the low post area and cover the corner or stay in the post and give up an uncontested shot by O2 or hope X3 can cover the corner.

Diagram 5

3. *Creating an Overload* (Diagrams 6 and 7). The triangle and box examples of overloading a zone are created by either dribbling the ball to the ball side or cutting a player to the ball side. Generally speaking, dribbling to the ball side from the point will shift and put the top of the zone at a disadvantage. Cutting a player along the baseline will shift the bottom of the zone, putting the opponent's normal coverage in question. It is a good idea to combine both cutting and dribbling to construct the overload. These concepts will both overload and distort the defense. One method of combining both the dribble and the cut is called *dribble pull,* which we will explain in detail later in this chapter.

Diagram 6

Diagram 7

TERM: BALL REVERSAL

Ball reversal simply means starting the ball on one side of the court and then moving it to the other side. Ball reversal is critical for any fundamental offense because it causes the zone to shift and takes the defensive players from the ball side and puts them on the help side of the floor. The quicker and more efficiently ball reversal can be done, the more difficult it is for the defense to adjust, often leaving the defenders out of position. I will describe five different methods to reverse the ball against a zone:

1. *Point Reversal* (Diagrams 8 and 9). Point reversal is the most obvious way to swing the ball, but often the most misused. Many times the point guard will follow his pass to the wing to the ball side, making it almost impossible to reverse the ball through him to the opposite wing without dribbling. Dribbling gives the defense more time to shift and adjust their positions and eliminates the advantage that would have been gained by a more efficient movement of the ball. Diagram 8 illustrates this incorrect method of reversal.

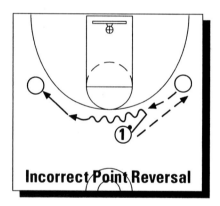

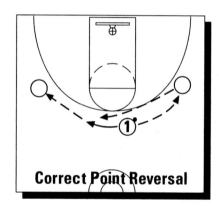

Diagram 8   **Diagram 9**

Instead, we instruct our point guard to "stay in the shoot." The "shoot" is the area of the court from the sides of the lane extended to half court, or the shaded area shown on the job description page for the point guard. Positioning the point guard to the far side of the shoot, closest to the help side, accomplishes three things that help in reversal: First, it keeps the defense from ganging up on the ball side. Second, it enables the point guard to have the correct angle to penetrate and pitch versus the top defender of the zone. Finally, it allows the ball to be reversed without the point guard having to dribble to improve his passing angle to the weakside wing. Diagram 9 shows the correct positioning of the point guard to reverse the ball.

2. High Post Reversal (Diagrams 10–14). Reversing the ball through the high post is the most effective of the five types of ball reversal. Having the ball in the high post makes the defense condense and turn to the middle of the floor, therefore immediately making the other four offensive players potential receivers. We try to reverse the ball through the high post as often as possible because of the pressure it puts on the defense and the passing opportunities it provides for the offense. What follows is a description of the four "looks" that we teach our players when they have caught the ball at the high post.

   a. The first look should always be to his "buddy," the other post player. The low post player could be on either side of the key, but for us, it is better if he is on the side opposite the high post. Diagram 10 shows the first look for the high post to reverse the ball. If the low post is opposite, there is a good chance he will occupy the help-side wing on the base of the zone. If he does, then the offside defensive guard is forced to cover both the wing and the point, giving us the two-on-one advantage we are always working to get.

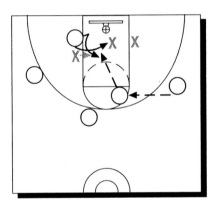

Diagram 10

   b. The second look is to the offside wing, who has moved "out of line" from the wing defender. Often this pass is not available when the wing players fail to get open because they are standing in a straight line with the ball and the defender. A step or two in either direction will open up the passing angle for a high post reversal. Diagram 11 shows a wing getting off the straight line, and Diagram 12 shows the high post reversal to the offside wing when defender X3 has taken away the first look by staying with O5 on his cut.

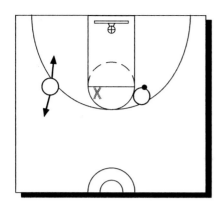

Diagram 11

Diagram 12

c. The third look for the high post would be to the point man, who follows his same rule of staying in the shoot and has taken the position above the opposite elbow from the high post man. This location puts the point guard in a position for either a shot, penetration or ball reversal to the wing (Diagram 13).

d. The fourth and final look for the high post to reverse the ball would be to the player who initially passed him the ball and who has relocated out of the line of the defense. This look would not be the first choice for many reasons—the main one being that the ball has stayed on the same side of the floor and is more of a kick-out pass than a reversal. Diagram 14 shows the high post taking his fourth option.

Diagram 13

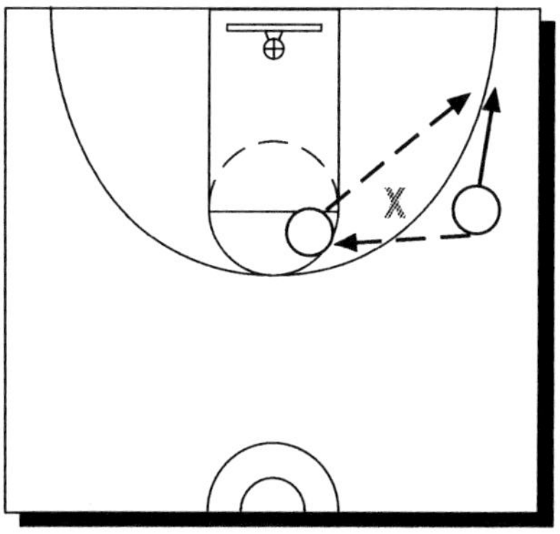

Diagram 14

When the ball has been passed to the high post area against a zone, the defense is the most vulnerable. High post reversal is a great option because it opens up all areas of the floor for the offense, allowing everyone on the floor to be an option and only a single pass away. This reversal stretches the defense and prevents the defenders from cheating on one player or favoring one side of the floor.

When we are practicing with our high post players on their looks, we have them back out and pump fake to each of their four options in sequence so it becomes instinctive. The more you drill your high post players to make their looks, the more proficient and effective passers they will become. Your post players have to work hard to cut, hold off and target the ball so that they are catching the ball as often as possible in the high post area. Remind your perimeter players that nothing makes the post people stop working like not getting the ball when they are open.

The following drills teach the passing sequence for the high post. They also show how to practice the shots that come from those passes.

High post flash and shoot—Player 1 flashes to the high post, receives the ball from the coach and turns and shoots while player 2 moves in for the offensive rebound on the weak side. Player 2 then passes the ball out and becomes the next player to flash and shoot, while player 3 moves in to rebound.

Diagram 15

High post flash and high-low pass—Player 1 flashes to the high post, catches the ball from the coach, turns and makes his first read (his buddy in the low post) and passes to O2, who has stepped over a dummy defender and calls for the ball. After passing, player 1 follows to the offensive board and rebounds any miss. Player 2 will be the next person to flash into the high post, and player 3 will step in for the dump-down pass.

Diagram 16

The second look of the high post is to the wing opposite. Player 1 flashes into the high post, catches a pass from the coach, turns and ball fakes to his first look (the low post) and then passes to player 6, who starts on the wing and goes out of line for the catch and shot. As soon as player 1 passes the ball to player 6, he goes to the weakside board for the rebound of any miss.

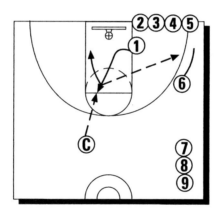

Diagram 17

This drill is the same as the previous drill, except it is run to the opposite side. You can also add the next post player stepping in to the low post and then going to the offensive boards along with the high post.

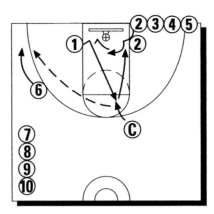

Diagram 18

This shooting drill uses the fourth option from the high post, the kick-out to the wing on the ball side. Player 1 flashes into the high post and catches the ball and goes through the first two options (high-low, wing opposite) and then kicks out to the wing on the ball side for the shot. Player 6 enters the ball and then moves out of line to receive the kick-out pass and shoot. Player 1 goes to the weakside offensive rebound position as soon as he passes.

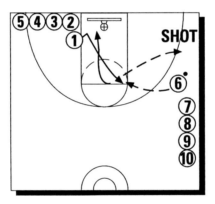

Diagram 19

This is the same drill on the other side of the court, except that we have added the first pass from the coach at the point. A dummy defender can be inserted between the coach and player 6, so that player 6 has to move out of line to receive the ball from the coach.

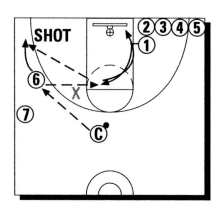

Diagram 20

The third look for the player in the high post is to pass back out to the point. This drill has the point receiving a pass from the coach on the wing, then feeding the player flashing into the high post and then offsetting in the shoot to receive the kick-out from the high post. As soon as the high post passes the ball out, he vacates and goes to the offensive boards.

The high post goes through his series of looks, starting with the low post, then continuing with the wing opposite and then the ball-side wing, before looking at the point. He can ball fake all those options before he passes out to the point.

Diagram 21

3. *Skip Reversal* (Diagrams 22 and 23). The skip pass is the quickest method of reversing the basketball across the court, because it "skips" one of the players on its way from side to side. For example, instead of the ball going from the wing to the point to the opposite wing, the ball goes directly across from wing to wing, skipping the point man completely. It has become a very popular method of reversing the ball against both man-to-man and zone defenses. Not long ago, a cross-court pass in basketball was considered a fundamental sin. We still try to avoid a flat skip pass that can be easily intercepted by the defense and is difficult for the receiver to catch and shoot because his

shoulders and feet are not in ready-shoot position on a flat pass. Diagram 22 provides an example of a flat skip pass.

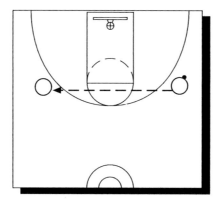

Diagram 22

Good passes are ones that lead to good shots. The less the receiver has to readjust his body and feet to catch and shoot, the greater chance the shot has of going in. For that reason, we prefer a diagonal skip pass that has some angle on it. It is important that the receiver always be above or below the line of the ball—preferably above. Being above the line of the ball enables the receiver to catch the ball with his shoulders square to the basket and release in a one-piece motion. Below is an example of a diagonal skip pass (Diagram 23).

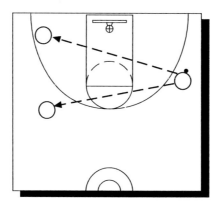

Diagram 23

4. *Dribble Reversal* (Diagrams 24 and 25). Reversing the ball with a dribble can be an effective way to attack some zones or isolate certain matchups to the advantage of the offense. The first thing dribbling will tell you about the zone is if it is using man-to-man principles. This can be detected if the man guarding the ball either stays with the dribbler, causing the zone to shift, or if the defensive man stays with the dribbler until he can pass him along to the next available defender. Below (Diagram 24) is an example of X2 passing the ball

handler to X1 as he crosses the floor with the dribble. We will use this maneuver if we want to make sure that X1 is matched up with our point guard, and not the wing man. This strategy becomes important if we want to isolate a particular post defender in our opponent's zone defense.

Another example of using the dribble to reverse the ball is what we term "fake dribble reversal." The dribbler takes the ball hard from the ball side to the help side and then quickly reverses and returns the ball with a pass to the side he just left. This is a good maneuver to use against a team that does a great job of sprinting to help. Diagram 25 is an example of a fake dribble reversal.

 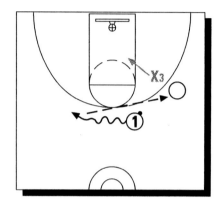

Diagram 24   **Diagram 25**

5. *Baseline Reversal* (Diagrams 26 and 27). The baseline reversal was an option my father's teams ran often and effectively. The only real problem with this method of reversal is the amount of space available on the baseline on some courts. A gym with a wall close to the baseline was a limiting factor.

    Diagram 26 shows how this method of reversing the ball was accomplished. O1 dribbled hard toward the baseline, forcing X5 to come and support X3 and not allow O1 to turn the corner for an easy basket. The goal was to occupy both X3 and X5 with the drive, which left X4 as the only remaining baseline defender. As X5 went to help, O4 screened in on X4 and O2 spotted up in the far corner. When O1 got to the baseline, he continued forward, jumping out of bounds while reading the reaction of X4. If X4 stayed screened, O2 was wide open in the corner. If X4 got over the screen, O4 slipped into the open area in the low past for the drop pass. I know it looks crazy, and I never believed it would work myself, but it has continued to work time after time.

    Other adjustments off of the same play that have been difficult for zones to defend are to put a post player in the low block, ball side, and then step him up the lane line while placing another shooter diagonally opposite (Diagram 27). Although you may be able to create other options, much of the success will depend on the ability of your dribbler to stay in the air and be able to make decisions while airborne.

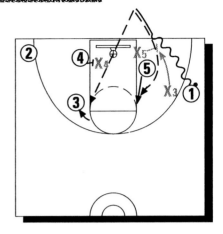

Diagram 26   **Diagram 27**

TERM: PENETRATE AND PITCH

Penetrate and pitch is the term we use for penetrating the zone with the dribble in an attempt to force a two-on-one opportunity or isolate a specific defender in a matchup of our choice. Anytime we can create a two-on-one situation against man-to-man or zone, it is to our advantage and considered good offense. In this section, I will describe four different types of penetrate and pitch.

1. *Two-on-One versus Baseline Players* (Diagram 28). As the ball is reversed through the point, O1 splits the defensive guards and attacks the basket. X5 must decide whether to rotate to help on O1 or stay with O5, whom he was matched up with before the penetration. Naturally, if X5 steps over to stop O1's penetration, the ball is dropped off to O5 for the power shot or dunk. If X5 holds his ground and tries to challenge O1's shot at the last second, he creates the best possible offensive situation. First of all, O1 may make the shot, but more important, O5 has been turned loose to go to the offensive glass with no one to block him out. This defensive strategy creates a good first shot and a better second shot if the first is missed. The offense should result in a score or foul whenever we can get into the center of the zone, with the ball in the hands of a good passer, and force help to come from the bottom of the zone.

2. *Two-on-One versus Perimeter Players* (Diagram 29). Using the techniques for point reversal discussed in the previous section, O1 offsets "in the shoot" so that when the ball is passed from O3, he is forcing a matchup with X2, and not X1. O1 then attacks X2 by driving right at him and forcing him to stop the ball. If X2 does not stop O1, then he continues into the paint, creating a two-on-one with the post, which we diagrammed on the previous page. As O1 drives at X2, O2 slides out of line with X2, either above or below the line of the ball. Now in a two-on-one situation, X2 must then decide if he is going to guard O1 or O2. If X2 commits to O1, then O2 should be open for a pass and a shot. The only way left for the defense to cover O2 is to bring X4 out of the low post to cover the

wing, again creating a two-on-one with 04 in the low post. Penetrate and pitch for a two-on-one against a perimeter player is accomplished by attacking the zone, as shown below.

The key to the success of the action shown here is getting 01 offset and away from the ball, bypassing X1 and forcing X2 to defend him. If X1 were to chase 01 all the way across the shoot, allowing X2 to cover the wing, you could see how much it would open up the entire high post area for an entry pass.

Diagram 28

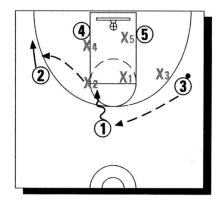

Diagram 29

3. *Penetrate and Pitch to Ensure a Post Attack* (Diagram 30). We can also us the same penetrate-and-pitch technique to force the bottom of the zone to shift and cover the wing by making a small adjustment with the wing involved in the two-on-one. This method is used when we want to ensure a specific matchup in the low post. The desire to get a particular matchup may be caused by one of their post defenders being in foul trouble or simply not being able to handle our player on the block. Diagram 16 shows how we set this up.

Diagram 30

The ball is reversed through the point guard, who has offset in the shoot. He once again drives the ball hard at X2, forcing him to stop the ball or give O1 penetration deep into the zone. As O1 drives, O2 slides out of line down to the baseline, leaving only X4 to come out and defend him. If X5 is the defender we are trying to isolate in the low post, we have successfully accomplished that by matching him up with O4.

The good zone coach will try to counter this move by letting his guards try to cover more territory or by having X2 bluff at O1, causing him to pick up his dribble so X2 can then slide over to cover O2. Anytime O1 doesn't offset correctly and allows himself to be played by X1, he will free up X2 to cover the wing and X4 to stay in the post, thus neutralizing what we are attempting to do. If O1 is offset correctly and X1 jumps clear across the floor to match up with him, once again, the high post area of the court will be unprotected.

4. *Penetrate and Pitch Using the Dribble Pull* (Diagrams 31 and 32). Dribble pull is a technique we use mainly from the offensive corner or wing positions. If the zone's rule is not to leave the dribbler, we can force the defender to vacate, or at least stretch his area while we cut another offensive player into the open spot. Diagram 31 shows an example of a "dribble pull" from the corner.

Diagram 31   **Diagram 32**

In the diagram above, O3 is being guarded in the corner by X3. O3 dribbles hard up the wing, forcing X3 to stay with him and vacating the corner area. As the corner opens up, O2 immediately fills the spot. By keeping O5 in the post, X5 must now decide whether he is going to stay in the post or cover O2 in the corner. If X5 holds in the post until O2 has caught the ball and then closes out to the corner, O5 simply turns and seals the next defender coming across and gets the post feed from O2.

Diagram 32 provides an example of a dribble pull from the wing. From the wing, O3 occupies X3 with a dribble back toward the top, while O2 uses a shallow cut into the vacant area. Shallow cutting the point can create advantageous mismatches for your offense.

DRILLS FOR PENETRATION AND PITCH

The point man drives between two defenders, one defender steps up to stop the penetration and the point passes to the wing on that side for a spot-up shot. The shooter on the other wing goes in for the offensive board, and the next three players step in to do the same sequence.

Diagram 33

The point man draws both defenders and passes out of the trap. The receiver catches and shoots, and the other wing follows for the offensive board. The next three players step in immediately to repeat the same sequence.

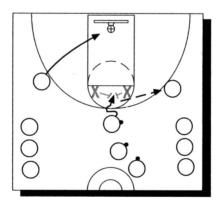

Diagram 34

The coach starts with the ball on the wing with X1 checking him. He passes to the point, who ball fakes to the other side and then splits the top two defenders and challenges X3 for the shot or the drop-off to player 2. If O1 gets the shot away, O2 gets inside position for the offensive put-back.

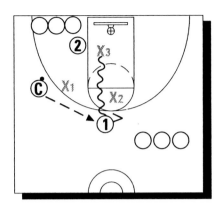

Diagram 35

Penetration and quick interior passing drill—Player 1 penetrates and draws both defenders to him. He then drops the ball off to either of the other two offensive players, who move out of line and attempt to get an open shot within no more than two passes. The two defenders involved in the trap stop playing once the ball has been passed out of the trap. This is an excellent drill to teach interior touch passing and movement, as well as offensive rebounding.

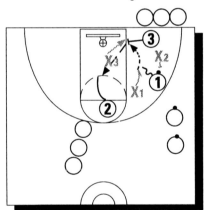

Diagram 36

Penetration and pitch and interior passing drill, 4-on-4—Versus a box defense, the point man drives the gap, drawing both defenders. He then passes the ball to one of the other three offensive players, who should all be moving to create passing lanes. As soon as the ball has been passed out of the trap O1, X1 and X2 all stop playing while O2, O3 and O4 take on the two remaining defenders (X3 and X4), trying to score in no more than two or three quick touch passes. The five players left to finish the drill can battle for the offensive rebound.

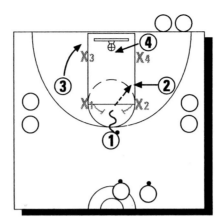

Diagram 37

This drill is the same as the previous one, except the penetration takes place from the wing. The drill can start with the coach passing the ball from the point, so he can go to either wing for penetration.

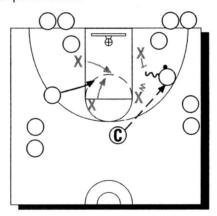

Diagram 38

4-on-4 penetration, pitch and interior passing drill versus a diamond—The concept here is the same as in the drill against a box defense, except with different angles of attack. The two defenders involved in the trap and the offensive player doing the dribble penetration all stop playing after the first pass, leaving O2, O3 and O4 to finish against X3 and X4.

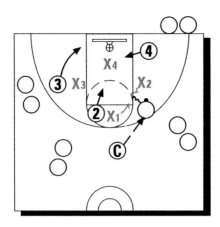

Diagram 39

4-on-4 penetration, pitch and interior passing versus a diamond zone from the baseline—The rules in this drill are the same as those in the previous three drills, except for a different angle to attack from, making the first pass out of the trap come up from the baseline.

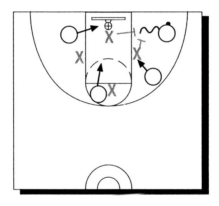

Diagram 40

TERM: DISTORTING THE ZONE

Distorting a zone is accomplished by aligning your offensive players in places that create confusion for the defenders on their coverage. Distorting the zone causes the defense to not line up where they normally would have guarded who they normally think they would. It is another method to create two-on-one situations. It can be as simple as playing two guards against a one-guard defensive front or one guard against a two-guard set. This idea is as old as basketball itself, but it is still effective because it puts a question into the minds of the defenders as to who is guarding whom.

It is interesting for the coach to distort zones with their initial setup to see how the defense is going to react. This distortion will provide valuable information on their coverages, and that will help the coach decide which sets will work best against them as the game progresses.

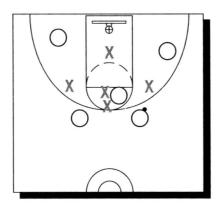

Diagram 41

Above (Diagram 41) is a simple distortion of a 1-3-1 zone. By placing two guards on top of the zone, the wing defenders are forced to match with one of the guards out front. This move, in turn, would cause the back defender to match up with a corner (wing) player, probably away from the ball. By moving them away from the area where they want to play and putting some doubt in their minds as to how far out of their area they should go, the offense has gained an advantage.

The following diagrams illustrate a number of other ways you can distort zones through your initial setup:

Two guards versus a one-guard front on top while you put three players (two offensive posts and a rover) versus two on the baseline (Diagram 42)

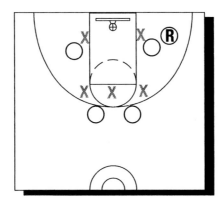

Diagram 42

A high post and two low posts versus two wing defenders and two post defenders (Diagram 43)

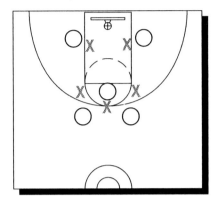

Diagram 43

Any kind of stack can initially distort the zone (Diagrams 44–49)

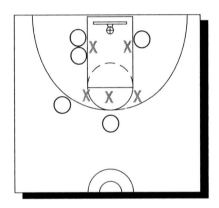

Diagram 44

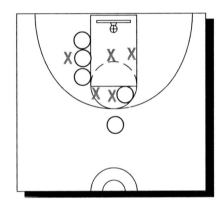

Diagram 45

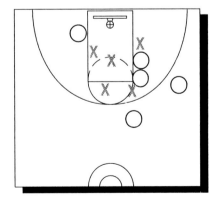

Diagram 46

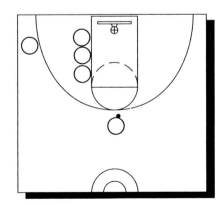

Diagram 47

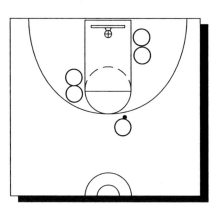

Diagram 48

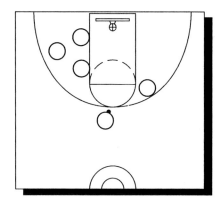

Diagram 49

CHAPTER 4

Entries and Quick Hitters

This chapter contains a series of entries that we use to distort zones and that we also use as "quick hitters." Quick hitters are offensive sets that allow the offense to get a good shot in a minimum amount of time and with just a few passes. We use them to speed up the game tempo or to score in a hurry when we are trailing late in the game.

A. QUICK HITTER—ENTRY TO THE RIGHT WING OUT OF A 1-4 SET.

A 1-4 set is especially good at relieving pressure because it immediately give us four receiver available for the entry pass.

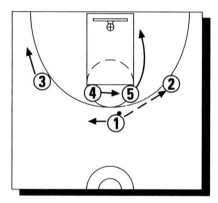

Diagram 50

O1

- Enters the ball to the right wing and goes opposite to the help side of the shoot

- Prepares himself for point ball reversal

O2

- Catches the ball and squares to the basket

- First look is to O5 cutting to the low post

- Second look is to feed O4 flashing into the high post

- Third look is to skip pass to O3

- Finally, he can reverse the ball through O1, who has offset in the shoot

O3
- Gets himself out of line to receive the skip pass

- If he gets the skip, his first look is to catch and shoot

O4
- Looks to flash into the high post just as O5 slides low and vacates the area

- Prepares to make the catch at the high post and make his four reads

O5
- Begins at the high post and slides low and posts hard, as soon as O2 catches the ball

B. QUICK HITTER—ENTRY TO THE RIGHT HIGH POST FROM A 1-4 SET

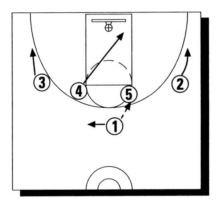

Diagram 51

O1
- Enters the ball to O5 and goes opposite to the help side of the shoot

- Prepares himself for a point ball reversal

O2
- Moves out of the line, toward the baseline

- If the pass comes to him, he can catch and shoot or feed the low post

O3
- Moves out of the line, away from the ball

- Readies himself to receive a pass and shoot

04

- Takes a quick diagonal dive to the opposite low post

- Posts hard after getting to the low post, calling for the ball and occupying at least one defender

05

- Receives the ball from O1 and backs out, using an inside pivot, so he can see the whole floor

- Makes his sequence of four looks

    —To his buddy in the low post

    —Wing opposite

    —Opposite elbow for point reversal

    —Same-side wing

C. QUICK HITTER—ENTRY TO THE RIGHT WING FROM A 1-4 SET.

A quick overload attack that gets a look at a three from the corner or a post feed to O5. The key is for O2 to set up low enough to occupy X3 when he receives the first pass.

Diagram 52

O1

- Favors O2's side to try to keep X2 occupied and help O2 draw X3 to him.

- Makes the entry pass to O2 and offsets for reversal

O2

- Sets up in the gap between X2 and X3, low enough that X3 has to match up with him, but high enough that X3 is not able to cover the corner

- Carries the threat of a shot to keep the defense honest

- Reads how X5 shifts as O3 and O4 cut to the overload

O3

- Makes a hard cut into the corner; he can go first if he wants to bring X5 to the corner and open up O4's cut to the post, or he can go after O4 if he wants to let X5 get matched up with O4

- Gets himself squared to the basket so he can catch shoot quickly

- Reads low post if X5 closes out on him

- Can kick back to O2 if X3 tries to cover the corner

O4

- Makes a hard diagonal cut and posts hard

- Helps O2 with the read by calling for the ball if X5 covers the corner

O5

- Occupies X2 by targeting the ball with his hands and voice when the ball is at the point

- Steps out and screens X2 so as not to allow him to slide down and cover O2

- Anticipates a shot when the ball gets into either O3 or O4 and goes weakside to rebound

D. QUICK HITTER—WEAKSIDE DOUBLE SCREEN OUT OF A 1-4 SET.

If you are trying to make the entry pass into the high post area, O2 and O3 can start in a little tighter and pop up and out to occupy the top defenders. This play will work against either a 2-3 zone or a 3-2 zone (Diagram 53)

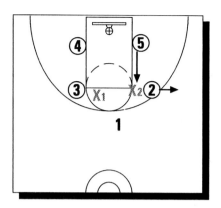

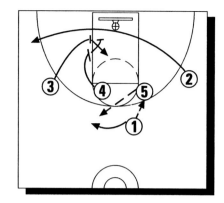

Diagram 53   **Diagram 54**

O1
- Ball fakes out to O2 to help open up the high post and then hits O5 as he cuts open

- Offsets in the shoot for a quick reversal

- Reads the defenders in the double screen to decide whether he is going to pass to O2 in the corner or look for the pop out of the stack

O2
- Hard cuts to the corner off the double screen

- Squares up at the end of the cut so he can catch and shoot

O3
- Sets low in the double screen with O4 on top

- Pops the stack by flashing hard into the key off O4's down screen after O2 has cleared the screen

O4
- Sets up in the double screen

- After O2 has cleared the screen, he screens down for O3

- Anticipates the shot and moves into position to rebound

O5
- Flashes into the high post to catch the entry pass

- Reverses the ball back to O1

- Anticipates the shot from the corner and rebounds weakside

E. QUICK HITTER—BALL SCREEN FOR POINT.

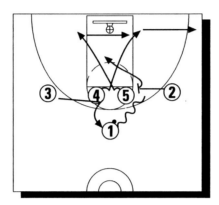

Diagram 55

O1
- Sets up screen by looking for the high post as they squeeze to the middle

- Uses his dribble to turn the corner in either direction

- Reads O4 on the diagonal post cut, then O2 rolling off the screen down the middle of the key; also looks for his shot while turning the corner

O2
- Lets O4 and O5 compress the top of the zone and then screens in on the top outside defender

- Rolls off the screen, looking for the return pass from O1

- Anticipates the shot and gets rebounding position

O3
- Screens in on the top of the zone like O2

- If O1 doesn't come to his side, he pops back out to the point for a release pass

O4
- Compresses the top of the zone by stepping to the middle of the foul line in a position to receive the ball

- If the dribbler goes away from him, he takes a hard diagonal cut to the low post on the ball side, looking for a pass from O1

- If he doesn't get the ball by the time he gets to the low post, O4 continues out to the corner to stretch the zone, catch and shoot, or feed O5 flashing to the post

O5

- Compresses the top of the zone the same as O4

- If the ball comes to his side, he takes a diagonal cut to the opposite low post

- As O4 clears to the corner, he cuts across the key to the ball-side post

F. QUICK HITTER—2-1-2 ENTRY.

We use the 2-1-2 entry versus most one-guard front zones. This entry distorts the zone initially and gives us good player movement quickly.

Diagram 56

O1

- Hits O4 on the wing

- Offsets to the opposite side of the shoot

O2

- Goes away to the opposite wing and gets himself out of line

- Prepares to catch and shoot or feed the post on a skip pass

O3

- Fills the high post area that has just been vacated by O5

- Flashes in under the defense so he can attack the basket on a catch

04

- Receives the ball from 01 and squares up to the basket

- Looks first to 05 cutting to the basket

- Next look is to 03 filling the high post

- Third, he can skip the ball to 02, who should be in a seam of the zone on the weak side

- Finally, he can reverse the ball back through the point

05

- Breaks hard to the low post area on the ball side

- Posts up strong, trying to get the ball or occupy any defender in that area

G. QUICK HITTER—TO GET THE BALL INTO THE HIGH POST FOR A HIGH-LOW TO 05.

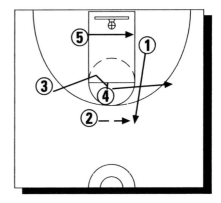

Diagram 57   **Diagram 58**

From a 2-3 set:
01

- Dribbles away from 02, then reverses and passes the ball back to 02

- Cuts directly down the lane in the seam between the top and the bottom of the zone

- If 04 receives the ball in the high post, he widens out so 05 can get a high-low pass

- If 04 does not receive the ball in the high post, he cuts back up the lane, gets the reversal from 02 and looks for 03 flashing into the high post vacated by 04

O2

- Receives the reversal from O1 and looks immediately for O4 filling the high post just vacated by O5

- If O4 is not open on his cut, he reverses the ball back to O1

O3

- Spots up on the three-point line to widen the top of the zone

- If O4 catches the ball in the high post, he fades to the corner, staying out of line

- If O4 does not receive the ball on his cut, he waits until the ball has been swung back to O1 and then flashes hard into the high post

- If he receives the ball in the high post, he goes through the sequence of looks, starting with the high-low to O5

O4

- Flashes into the high post as O1 passes to O2

- If he receives the ball, he goes through his four looks, starting with a high-low to O5

- Vacates the high post back to the wing when O2 passes back to O1 and fades to the corner if O3 catches at the high post

O5

- Goes low post opposite as soon as O1 reverses the ball to O2

- Stays in the low post, waiting for the ball to be caught in the high post so he can step in for the high-low pass

H. QUICK HITTER—PENETRATION AND CUT FROM THE WING VERSUS A 3-2 ZONE.

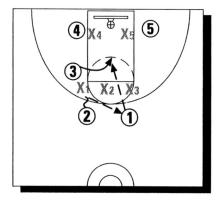

Diagram 59

01
- Receives the pass from 02 and attacks the gap between X2 and X3

- Attempts to draw both defenders to him as high as possible

- Drops the ball over the top of the zone to 03 cutting in from the wing

- Moves so he is out of the line in case 03 needs a release

02
- Tries to occupy X1 and draw X2 by faking penetration in their gap

- If he can draw X2 even one step, it will help 01 by producing a bigger gap between X2 and X3

- Reverses the ball to 01

03
- Waits until 01 starts his penetration and then cuts behind the top of the zone, into the seam

- Catches and goes 3-on-2 versus the bottom two defenders

04 and 05
- Occupy their men on the baseline

- As soon as the ball is received by 03, they prepare for a quick drop pass if their man helps

- Get inside rebounding position if 03 takes the ball to the basket, anticipating a miss

CONTINUATION OF PENETRATION AND CUT FROM THE WING VERSUS A 3-2 ZONE:

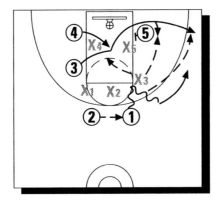

Diagram 60

44

O1

- If O3 is not open on his first cut into the middle of the zone, O1 backs the dribble out, favoring X3's side

- First look is for O3 curling off O5's screen or continuing to the corner

- Second look is for O5 slipping the screen to the basket

- Third look is for O4 flashing into the middle of the key; this one will be open if X4 slides across to help on O3's cut or to cover for X5 if he goes to the corner

O2

- Same responsibilities as those described on previous page.

O3

- If not open on his initial cut to the middle, he goes off O5's screen and can either curl for the short jumper or go to the corner for the three

- Can also feed the post if X5 comes out to the corner with him

O4

- If O3 gets the ball in the corner or the curl, he should anticipate a shot and get position

O5

- Screens X5 from the outside as O3 continues his cut

- Can slip the screen and get a pass from O1 or post up if O3 gets the ball in the corner

I. QUICK HITTERS–"J" CUT FROM A 1-2-2 SET.

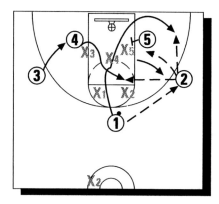

Diagram 61

01

- This play can be designed for your best perimeter shooter, who can run this set from O1's position, and can be run in either direction

- Passes to O2

- Splits the top defenders and can look for a quick return pass as soon as he is below the top of the zone

- If he doesn't get the pass in the middle of the zone, he continues to the baseline and curls off the low post on the ball side

- Thinks shot, low post feed or high post feed

02

- Receives the entry pass and looks for O1 in the middle of the zone or curling out to his side

- Reads how X5 plays the curl and can pass to O5 slipping the screen or posting

- If he passes to either O1 or O5, he must move out of the line for a return pass

03

- Moves down the low post vacated by O4 and gets rebound position

04

- Allows O1 to split the middle of the zone, and then, as he clears, flashes to the high post

05

- Screens X5 from the outside and lets O1 read the defender

- If X5 has moved up to cover O2 on the initial pass, he would screen X4, which would make the play more effective

- Can slip the screen or post up after O1 has cleared

J. QUICK HITTER—JUMPER OFF A BASELINE DOUBLE OUT OF A 1-2-2 SET.

Diagram 62

O1

- Enters the ball to O2

- Offsets to the far side of the shoot

O2

- Catches and ball fakes to the low post or middle of the zone to compress the defense

- Reverses the ball to O1

- Goes to the weakside board, anticipating a shot after the reversal

O3

- Comes down to set a double screen with O4 on the block

- Sets a screen for O4 after O5 has cleared the double

O4

- Sets the double with O3

- After O5 has cleared the double, he pops the stack off of O3's screen and quick flashes into the key

O5

- Posts up as O2 catches the initial pass

- Waits until the ball is reversed to O1 and then cuts hard off the bottom of the double, looking for jumper or post feed

K. QUICK HITTER—COMPANION PLAY FOR PREVIOUS PLAY.

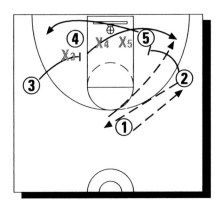

Diagram 63

O1

- Initiates the play as shown in Diagram 62

- As he receives the reversal, he ball fakes to the double screen and comes back to O3 coming off O2's screen on the original ball side

O2
- After he reverses the ball back to O1, he comes down to the baseline and screens X5, who has hedged over to help on the double

- After screening, he can post or pop out to the open area on the perimeter

O3
- Moves down to set the double with O4

- Pretends to be screening down for O4 to pop the stack and then cuts hard across the key, using O2's screen to get open in the corner

O4
- Sets the double screen with O3 for O5

- Gets into offensive rebounding position, waiting for the shot from O3

O5
- Waits for the reversal and then cuts hard off the double and calls for the ball

- After the pump fake from O1, he goes to the offensive boards, anticipating a shot from O3

L. QUICK HITTER—QUICK SCREEN FOR HIGH POST OUT OF A 2-2-1 SET.

This whole entry is run to attack the top of the zone using a 2-2-1 set:

Diagram 64

O1
- Enters the ball to O2 as he pops off the high post

- Goes away to fill the spot just vacated by O3

- Spots up for a second look from O3 if he catches the ball at the high post

O2
- Times his pop out of the high post

- Tries to hit O3 flashing into the high post

- If the pass goes into the high post, he moves laterally to become O3's fourth option out of the high post

O3
- Flashes into the high post, looking for the pass from O2

- If he receives a pass in the high post, he turns and faces the basket and goes through his four options (Diagram 64)

O4
- If O3 catches the ball in the high post, he moves down and gets out of line as O3's third option

O5
- Anticipates O3 catching the ball and begins to set up the defender for the quick flash into the key as O3's first option

CONTINUATION OF QUICK HITTER L FROM PREVIOUS PAGE.

If O3 is not open on his initial cut into the high post, the player action is as follows:

Diagram 65

O1
- Moves down to the spot vacated by O3 and spots up

O2
- Dribbles back toward the middle of the shoot

- Reverses and hits O3 stepping out from the screen

O3
- Holds his position hard in the high post to occupy his defender, whether it is X2, who has dropped back, or X3 who has moved up

- Anticipates O2 reversing his dribble and cuts off O4's screen into shooting position

O4
- As O2 starts his dribble back to the middle, O4 sets a back screen on the player defending O3 in the high post

O5
- Anticipates O3's shot coming off the screen and rebounds weakside

M. QUICK HITTER—OUT OF A DOUBLE STACK VERSUS A 2-3 ZONE.

Diagram 66

O1

- Initiates the play with an entry pass into O5 popping out of the stack

- Sets up for a return pass out of line

O2

- Starts on the top of the stack

- Moves out to the weakside three-point line for a possible skip pass from O5 or O4

O3

- Makes a quick cut to the ball-side short corner and occupies X5

- As the ball gets returned to O1, O3 sets a double on the middle defender (X4) in the 2-3 zone

- Goes weakside for the rebound after screening

O4

- Holds in the low post as O5 pops out of the stack

- Moves up slightly to ensure that X4 is checking him

- Waits for the double screen to form and then curls off the screen for the shot

O5

- Pops out of the stack to receive the entry pass from O1 high enough to occupy X2

- Returns the ball to O1 and then sets a double screen with O3 on the middle defender in the zone

N. QUICK HITTER—DRIBBLE INTO A QUICK OVERLOAD SET.

We would use this set to isolate a specific zone defender in the low post or to drag a team's best rebounder away from the basket to cover our shooter in the corner. Nothing fancy, just "let's see how you are going to cover this" before we start our regular movement.

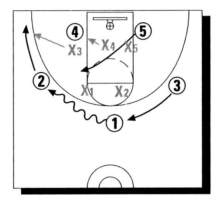

Diagram 67

01
- Dribbles at 02 and drives him into the corner

- Reads how the defense covers the overload, understands who the coach is trying to isolate and goes right at him if we have an advantage

02
- Keeps his spacing as 01 dribbles at him

- Sets up for a three from the corner

- Also needs to understand who we are trying to isolate

03
- Rotates to the point for a possible release pass if going into a regular zone offense

04
- If we are trying to isolate the middle defender in the bottom of the zone, he needs to see how the zone has shifted so he knows who is checking him

- If he has the isolation he wants, he works as hard as possible to get the ball and attack

05
- Starts weakside and flashes into the high post to form the overload set

- Needs to understand who we are isolating and get the ball to the correct person with either a high-low pass or a kick-out pass

O. QUICK HITTERS—ATTACKING A 1-3-1 WITH A QUICK OVERLOAD.

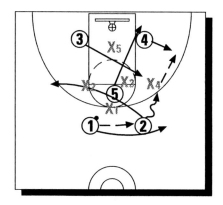

Diagram 68

O1
- Initiates the play by swinging the ball to O2

- Delays and then follows his pass as O2 vacates

- Sets up for a return pass

O2
- Receives the ball from O1, dribbles toward X3 to occupy him and hits O4 popping to the wing

- Shallow cuts through to the weakside wing and spots up

O3
- Starts low and opposite

- Flashes into the high post as O5 vacates

- Looks to receive the pass and attack with high post options

O4
- Pops out into the gap as X2 moves up toward O2

- Receives the pass and looks low to O5 sliding in where he just left, to O3 flashing into the high post

- If neither is easy, he reverses the ball back to O1

O5

- Slides low out of the high post and into the ball-side low post as the ball gets entered to O4

- Posts hard and occupies the bottom man on the 1-3-1 (X5)

- Looks for a high-low if O3 catches the ball flashing to the high post

CONTINUATION OF QUICK HITTER O FROM PREVIOUS PAGE.

If the defense shifts and covers the initial cuts, then the skip pass should be available against a 1-3-1 zone:

Diagram 69

O1

- Has followed the ball to the strong side and set himself in a position to receive a return pass out from O4

- As he receives the pass, he reads what the bottom defender X5 has done; he will either go with O5 across the key or stay in the low post with O3, who is filling from the high post

- He makes the read and passes to either O3 or O5

- O2 is available for the skip pass if X2 has dropped to help X5

O2

- Spots up, ready to catch and shoot on a skip pass

O3

- As the ball gets passed back out to O1, O3 quickly cuts into the low post area vacated by O5 and looks for a quick entry pass

O4

• Returns the ball to O1 and gets ready to go to the offensive board

O5

• As the ball is returned to O1, he quickly cuts across the key and looks for an opening in the bottom of the zone for the quick skip pass from O1

P. QUICK HITTER—2 REVERSALS FOR THE JUMPER VERSUS A 1-3-1.

Diagram 70

O1

• Lags behind O2 out of line of X1

• Catches the reversal from O2 and swings the ball quickly to O3

• Cuts hard to the basket, looking for a give-and-go

• Curls out the weak side off O5's screen for the shot

O2

• Penetrates with the ball to draw X1 and X4

• Reverses the ball to O1

• Follows his pass for the return pass from O3

• Receives the pass and swings the ball to O1 curling off O5's screen

O3

• V-cuts and gets out of line from X2 so that O1 can pass him the ball

• Catches and carries the threat of a shot while looking at O1 for a possible give-and-go

- Rebounds weakside with O5

O4
- Fills the high post area vacated by O5 as the ball is caught by O3

O5
- Starts at the high post and slides low and opposite when O3 receives the pass from O1

- Screens for O1 on X5 as the ball gets passed back to O2

- Can slip the screen

- Goes to the weakside rebounding position with O3

Q. QUICK HITTER—J-CUT AND SKIP PASS VERSUS A 1-3-1 ZONE.

Diagram 71

O1
- Crosses the ball to O2 and readies himself to become a release outlet if O4 can't make the skip pass.

O2
- Receives the ball from O1 and hits O4, who has J-cut down the lane and off O5's screen

- Takes a diagonal cut through the lane and goes to the weakside baseline, looking for the gap behind X5 and under X2

- Prepares to catch and shoot

O3
- As soon as the ball is entered to O4, he screens the most dangerous defender on the back side of the zone to free up O2 for the skip

O4

- J-cuts down the lane as soon as O1 prepares to pass to O2

- Comes off O5's screen and looks to shoot

- Skips the ball across the court to O2

- Can also look into O5 if X5 chases O2

O5

- Sets a screen on X5 for O4 to curl out the ball side

- Turns and posts up as O4 catches the ball in order to occupy X5

- Rebounds the weak side after the ball has been skipped to O2

R. QUICK HITTER—2-ON-1 SKIP PASS FOR A THREE VERSUS A 1-3-1.

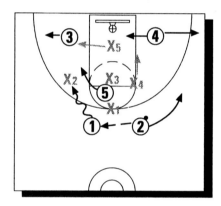

Diagram 72

O1

- Receives the pass across from O2 and drives right past the outside shoulder of X2

- Looks for O5 sliding into the seam between X2 and X3

- Looks for O3 stepping out on the baseline

- Makes the easier of the two decisions

O2

- Crosses the ball to O1 and goes away and spots up behind the three-point line for the skip pass

O3

- Starts just outside the low post area and drags X5 with him as he steps out to receive a pass from O1

- If X5 doesn't honor his cut, O3 prepares to catch and shoot

- If he receives the ball, he looks across court for O4 ducking in behind X5 and below X4, or for either O2 or O4 on the three-point line

O4

- Sets up just off the low block and reads how X5 plays O3 and how X4 plays O2

- If X5 leaves with O3 and X4 doesn't cover down, he goes to the basket

- If X4 covers down, he steps back to the three-point line and waits for the skip pass

O5

- As O1 dribbles at X2, he slides into the seam between X2 and X3, looking for a pass

- If he receives the pass, he looks low for O3 or O4 or backside for O2

S. QUICK HITTER—ATTACKING A 1-3-1 WITH BASELINE PENETRATION.

Diagram 73

O1

- Catches the pass from O2 and dribbles at X2 to create the opening for O2 on the baseline

- Passes to O2 and gets out of line for the return pass

02

• Swings the ball to 01 and takes a hard diagonal cut to the ball-side corner

• Catches the ball from 01 and attacks X5 with a dribble as he closes out

• Has a 2-on-1 read with 05 and can hit 04 is X3 slides down

03

• As soon as 02 catches the ball in the corner, he sets a screen up on X3 (the defender who normally would cover down on 05)

04

• Exchanges places with 05 by flashing to the high post as soon as 02 starts his cut

• Occupies X3, or calls for the ball if X3 drops down to help on the penetration

05

• Vacates the high post as the ball is swung to 01

• Prepares to play 2-on-1 with 02 against X5

T. QUICK HITTER—HIGH POST J-CUT OR SKIP PASS VERSUS A 1-3-1 ZONE.

Diagram 74

01

• Enters the ball to 03 and fills the spot vacated by 02

• Spots up for the skip pass and a three-point shot

02

• Slides out of line, down to the baseline, outside the three-point line

- Spots up and looks for the skip pass from O3

O3

- Positions himself to catch the entry pass and occupy X4

- Reads the ball-side baseline screen, looking for O5 on the curl or O4 slipping the screen

- Watches to see which other defender drops to help on the action with O4 and O5, and if they are defended, he skips the ball to either O1 or O2 for the three

O4

- Steps in and screens X5 as O5 takes his J-cut

- Can slip the screen if there is no other defensive help

- Otherwise, he rebounds weakside for the skip pass and the three-point shot

O5

- J-cuts out of the high post on the pass from O1 to O3

- Curls off the screen, looking for the jumper or the 2-on-1 with O4

- Can also skip the ball to O1 or O2

U. QUICK HITTER—SLASHING ATTACK VERSUS A 1-3-1 ZONE.

Diagram 75

O1

- Enters the ball to O3 and fills his position as he cuts through

O2

- Moves to the point and fills the area vacated by O1

O3

- Receives the pass from O1 and passes to O5 stepping out to the short corner

- Makes a hard cut to the basket, looking for a give-and-go

- Continues his cut to the block on the weak side

O4

- Starts at the high post and cuts to the basket, trailing O3 and looking for a gap created by O3's cut

- Posts up on the low block

O5

- Starts in the low post and steps out to the short corner to draw X5 away from his area

- Looks for O3 on a hard slashing give-and-go cut and then for O4 cutting right behind him

- Can look to O4 on the block if he has an advantage

- Reverses the ball to O1

CONTINUATION OF QUICK HITTER U—BALL REVERSAL.

Diagram 76

O1

- Gets himself out of line so that O5 can reverse the ball back to him

- Swings the ball back to O2 and spots up on the three-point line

O2

- Catches the reversal pass from O1 and looks for O5 flashing into the gap in the high post or O4 coming off the weakside screen set by O3 on the base of the zone

O3

- Waits on the weakside low block until the ball is swung from O1 to O2; he then screens the baseline defender for O4 to get open

O4

- Holds in the post until the ball is being passed to O2 at the point, and then he curls off the screen set by O3 on the weakside block

- Can look to shoot or attack 2-on-1 with the dribble

O5

- Reverses the ball back through O1 and immediately fills the gap in the high post area for a catch and shot or to read the options from the high post.

V. QUICK HITTER—SCREEN THE BACKSIDE AND DIAGONAL PASS VERSUS A 1-3-1 ZONE.

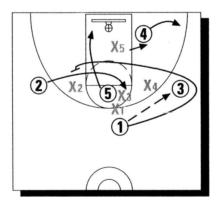

Diagram 77

O1

- Enters the ball to O3 and takes a quick cut to the outside of O3 and curls back across the middle of the key to the weak side

- As O3 ball fakes to O4, he back screens X2 to prevent him from dropping down to cover O5

O2

- As O1 starts curling back into the middle, he flashes into the high post just vacated by O5

- If he catches the ball there, he goes through the four high post options

- If O gets the ball, he rebounds weakside

03
- Receives the entry pass, and then, as 01 cuts around him, he ball fakes to 04 in the short corner

- After the ball fake, he looks first for 05 slicing down to the opposite low block or for 02 flashing into the high post

04
- As 03 catches the ball, he steps out to the short corner and calls for the ball to occupy X5 and draw him away from the basket

05
- As 01 starts his cutback into the middle, he checks X5 to see if he is going out with 04 and the ball fake. If so, he slices down the back side of the key, looking for a quick pass from 03

W. QUICK HITTER—PERIMETER PENETRATION VERSUS A 1-3-1 ZONE.

Diagram 78

01
- Enters the ball to 03 and slow cuts to the foul line

- As soon as 03 has dribbled and drawn the defense, he accelerates to the basket, looking for the pass from 03

02
- As 03 catches the ball, he cuts into the high post from behind and sets a brush screen on X3, just delaying him from dropping down to cover 01 or help on 04 and 05

O3

- Catches the entry pass and immediately drives over the top of X4, trying to get into the gap between X4 and X3

- Reads how X5 is defending and makes the easy pass to either O4 on the curl, O1 on the slice cut or O5 slipping the screen

O4

- As O3 catches the entry pass, O4 cuts across the key and curls off O5's screen, looking for the shot or a 2-on-1 attack

O5

- Screens for O4 as he crosses the key and looks to slip the screen or offensive rebound

X. QUICK HITTER—SECOND CUTTER ON A STACK ENTRY VERSUS A 3-2 ZONE.

Diagram 79

O1

- Crosses the ball to O2 and cuts hard down the seam of the zone, looking for a return pass

- Curls off of O4 to the corner to get a pass from O2

O2

- Catches the pass from O1 and looks for O1 cutting down the middle of the zone

- Second look is for O5 stepping out of the stack and then curling back in across the zone

- Third look is for O5 on the skip pass behind O3's screen

- As soon as he passes, he sets himself out of line for the kick-out pass (especially if X3 drops in coverage)

O3
- Waits until O5 and O1 have cut and then screens in on X4 so O5 can receive a skip pass from O2

O4
- Screens in on X5 first for O5 and then again for O1

- Goes to the offensive boards

O5
- Steps out of the stack, looking for the jumper or for penetration and kick-out

- If he doesn't receive the pass on the ball side, he goes across the lane off O3's screen and looks for the skip pass from O2

Y. QUICK HITTER—QUICK 3-ON-2 FOR A GREAT GUARD AGAINST AN ODD-FRONT ZONE.

Diagram 80

O1
- Receives the pass from O2; if X1 goes out with O3, he penetrates the gap, pulling X2 further toward the ball side and then hitting O2 on his cut to the basket

- If X1 doesn't go out to cover O3, then O1 passes to O3 for the shot or the feed to O2

O2
- This play is intended to use this guard's ability to catch and finish

- He swings the ball to 01 and then waits briefly for X2 to widen toward the ball

- He then cuts hard down the middle, slowing in the seam between the top and the bottom of the zone, looking for the return pass from either 01 or 03

- Plays out the 3-on-2 situation with 04 and 05

03
- Starts in the high post and steps out as 01 receives the pass from 02

- Tries to stretch X1 out with him as far as possible

- If he gets the pass from 01, his first read is 02 in the heart of the defense; his next read is a shot

04
- Stays high enough to occupy X3 and widen out the top of the zone

- As soon as 02 cuts down the middle of the zone, 04 cuts outside to be the third offensive player in the 3-on-2

05
- Occupies X4 and then plays 3-on-2 with 04 and 02

CONTINUATION OF QUICK HITTER Y.

Diagram 81

01
- Spots up and is a threat to catch and shoot a three

02
- If he doesn't get the ball on the cut down the middle, he continues on to the baseline and curls hard off the screen set by 05

- As soon as he catches the ball, he thinks "take it to the basket with the dribble" and creates the same 3-on-2 situation; he can drive over the top or the baseline

- His cut down the heart of the zone should have compressed the zone and made the screen on X4 easy for O5

O3
- Occupies X1 so he can't drop to the corner and help on the curl by O2

- Hits O2 as soon as he has cleared the screen

O4
- Stays in the opposite low block, thinking rebound or 3-on-2 with O2 and O5

O5
- Steps in to set a screen on X4 and then plays 3-on-2 when O2 catches the ball in the corner

Z. QUICK HITTER—SCREENING THE SLIDER IN A 1-2-2 ZONE FOR A LOB.

One of the keys to running an effective zone offense is the ability to understand how each zone shifts. This quick hitter is an example of how to take advantage of the knowledge that we have that says the way this team covers the corner is that the two baseline defenders slide over and to the top of the zone on the back side (X3) and down to the opposite low post.

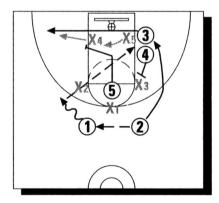

Diagram 82

O1
- Receives the pass from O2 to initiate the movement of the rest of the players

- Dribbles outside X2, looks to the cutters to the ball side O3 and O5 as they fill the corner and low post

- Next, he lobs up to O2, who is cutting off O4's back screen

O2

- Moves out to occupy X3, waits at his level and then cuts hard off the back screen for the lob

O3

- Makes a hard cut to the strongside corner, forcing the corner coverage by X4

O4

- As O3 and O5 are cutting, O4 sets a back pick on X3, the defender who is responsible for dropping on the weak side

O5

- On the pass from O2 to O1, O5 begins his cut down the middle and over to the low post to force the corner coverage by X5 and open up the weak side for the screen and the lob.

CHAPTER 5

Offensive Sets and Continuity Against Zone Defenses

Your zone offense should not require a great amount of adjustment from your regular offense. The closer you are in terminology and technique between the two offenses, the easier it will be for your players to learn their responsibilities and to carry over that knowledge into game action. Even though, if time permitted, a coach could design a special offense for every possible zone his team might see during the season, he is better off and more realistic to design offenses that fit his personnel and allow him to use and teach the same fundamentals his players are accustomed to utilizing.

All zone sets need to have purposeful player and ball movement. They should take into consideration the players' knowledge of gaps, penetration, overloading, spacing, creating matchups and ball reversal. The majority of what we do eventually ends up in a 1-3-1. We like this set because it provides strong rebounding and consistent defensive balance, with the point guard responsible for the first line of transition defense.

In this chapter, we are going to cover eight types of zone sets (plus options). Most of the fundamentals and terminology were used during the discussion of quick hitters in Chapter 4. Although no one can use all of these ideas, we encourage you to look closely at your personnel to decide which of these zone ideas will prove successful for your team this season. (Note: In the sections that describe each player's rules, or responsibilities, key terms are italicized.)

A. *REGULAR*

Diagram 83

This is what we call our basic 1-3-1 alignment, which has been effective for us for a number of years now (Diagram 83).

(Note: In the following explanation of the rules, or responsibilities, for each position, key terms are italicized.)

01
- Can pass the ball to any of the other positions and then relocate to the offside, but stays in the shoot

- Looks to keep reversing the ball, but has the freedom to penetrate and pitch

- Has the green light to penetrate and create, as long as he is under control

- Never shoots the ball from the straight-on angle at the top of the circle because it is the least predictable rebound angle and our rebounders cannot anticipate where the ball is coming off

02
- Plays the wing area or overloads to the corner

- Goes through anytime he passes the ball anywhere but the low post

- If he passes the ball to the low post area, he relocates out of line

- Must constantly be looking to feed the players in the post area

- Rebounds opposite on any shot taken

- Looks to execute the dribble pull maneuver with 03

- Looks to exploit gaps in the middle of the zone by cutting into the heart of the zone

- Can occasionally start through the zone and come back out ball side

03
- Plays the wing area or overloads to the corner

- Goes through anytime the ball is passed anywhere but the low post

- Must look to feed either post frequently

- Rebounds opposite on any shot

- Looks to execute the dribble pull maneuver with O2

- Looks to exploit any gaps in the middle of the zone by cutting into the heart of the zone and looking to receive the ball

- Relocates if he feeds the low post, making sure to stay out of line

O4
- Makes himself available to receive the ball back from the point or either wing

- Must keep his shoulders square to the ball

- We like him underneath the defensive guard, instead of in front of him

- When the ball is caught in the high post, he looks at his four options:

  —Buddy in the low post

  —Opposite wing

  —Opposite elbow

  —Same-side wing

- Always rebounds opposite

O5
- Posts up strong on the block

- Tries to collapse the defense by catching the ball

- After catching, he must keep a body on people to occupy them

- Can either follow the ball from side to side or stay

- Automatically ducks into the key when the high post catches the ball for the high-low

- Can step out to the short corner

- May screen for O2 and O3

- Rebounds the ball wherever it goes

B. CORNER OPTION

Diagram 84

O1

- Passes the ball to O3 on the wing

- Goes away to the far side of the shoot for a reversal

O2

- Flashes to the high post as soon as O5 rolls to the basket

- Looks for a gap in the high post area

- Looks to catch, shoot, attack the basket or follow the sequence of four passing options

O3

- Catches the ball and squares to the basket

- Passes the ball to O4, who has popped out to the corner

- He then makes a basket cut, looking for the ball

- If he doesn't receive the ball on the cut, he continues *on to the other side*

O4

- Catches *the ball and squares* to the basket

- Looks *at O3 to see if he* is open cutting to the basket

- He then looks to O5 cutting down the lane to the low block

- He then looks to O2, who has flashed into the high post

- If none of these options is open, he returns the ball to O1, who will come as far back as he needs to in order to meet the ball

05

- Flashes from *the high post* to the low post off O3's tail

- Stays on the low block, posting hard and trying to occupy any defender in the post

CORNER OPTION—CONT.

Diagram 85

01

- Comes as far back to the ball as necessary to receive the *pass from O4*

- Takes two hard dribbles toward the other *side of the* floor, forcing the defense to sprint *that way*

- Looks for O5 posting up

- Reverse pivots and looks for O2, who has stepped out of the post to the wing

- Returns to the opposite side of the shoot after the *pass for a* possible reversal

02

- Waits for the defense to shift

- Steps out to the wing against the flow of the defense

- Readies himself *for the jump shot*

- Looks to feed the ball to O4, *who has pulled* back to post up

O3
- Spots up on the weak side, ready to shoot if the defense doesn't shift quickly

- Stays out of line with the defense

O4
- Passes the ball out of the corner to O1 and starts *back across the* floor

- As O1 takes his two hard dribbles away, O4 reverse pivots as O2 catches the ball

- He posts hard, looking to receive the ball from O2

O5
- Goes from block to block as O1 takes his dribbles, and is the first option for O1

- He curls up to the ball a little *to create* a better angle and puts his body on the defender

- Rebounds the back side

This *offense has proven to be* an effective continuation series for us. We *get open three-pointers* and post-ups by throwing the ball back against *the flow of the defense.*

CORNER OPTION + HOLD

Diagram 86

01

- Enters the ball to 02

- Goes *to the far side* of the shoot for reversal

02

- Catches the ball and squares to the basket

- *Passes the* ball to 04, who has popped out to the corner, or

- Passes the ball *to 03, who has* flashed into the low post area

- Holds on the wing to form a box overload situation

- Keeps spacing while moving to an open gap for either a shot or a post feed

03

- Flashes into the low post as soon as 04 vacates the area

- Posts hard trying to seal the middle man in the zone, or

- Pins and looks for a high-low pass from 05

04

- Pops out to the corner

- Catches the ball and squares to the basket

- First look is to 03 flashing into the low post

- Second look is to 05 in the high post

- Third look is to 01 with a skip pass to the opposite elbow

- Final look is to the ball-side wing, 03, who has relocated with proper spacing and out of line of the defense

05

- Positions himself at the high post, looking to receive the ball from either the wing or the corner

- Keeps his shoulders square to the ball at all times

- If he receives the ball, he looks to score or feed the low post

C. POINT THROUGH OR "J" CUT

Diagram 87   **Diagram 88**

O1
- Makes the entry pass to O2 on the right wing and cuts through to either side

- If he comes to the *ball side, we have* box overload

- If he empties out the weak side, he looks to receive the reversal pass from O3

- If he gets the reversal pass, he has the option to shoot or dribble pull for O3, who has run through from the point (Diagram 88)

O2
- Receives the pass from O1 and squares to the basket

- If O1 makes a ball-side cut, O2 can execute a dribble pull with him

- He can feed O5 in the low post

- He can feed O4 in the high post for the pin and seal high-low pass

- He can reverse the ball through O3, who has moved to the point

O3
- Fills the point that was vacated by O1

- Stays on the far side of the shoot for a reversal

04

- Stays in the high post and calls for the ball

- If he receives the ball in the high post, he makes his high post reads

- Can X cut with 05 on a reversal (Diagram 88)

- Shoulders stay square to the ball

- Attempts to post beneath the top of the zone

- Rebounds weakside

05

- Posts strong and can screen and post if 01 cuts to his side

- Attempts to catch the ball and collapse the zone

- Can occasionally step out to the short corner

- Always looking for the high-low pass from 04

D. WRINKLE

As with many of our zone offenses, we prefer to start this series with a ball reversal to get the defense moving. The reversal is depicted in *Diagram 89*.

Diagram 89

01

- *Enters* the ball to 03 and makes a V-cut away from the pass

- Reverse pivots and comes back to the ball

- Swings the ball to 02

O2

- Waits for the ball to be swung back to him through O1

- Passes to O3, who has cut through to the corner

- Shallow cuts back to the spot vacated by O3

O3

- Receives the initial pass and then reverses it back to O1

- Cuts through the zone to the ball-side corner

- Receives pass from O2

O4

- Starts on the high post strongside and then goes with the ball on the reversal to the other high post

- Can X-cut with O5 on a reversal

O5

- Stays in the low post ball-side until the ball is reversed

- Moves across the key to the ball-side low post

- Can X-cut with O4 on a reversal

At this point, we have reversed the ball and moved the defense. Our main pattern is described in the next section (Diagram 90).

WRINKLE—CONT.

Diagram 90

01

- Relocates after the reversal on the far side of the shoot

- Gets a diagonal skip pass from O5

- Catches, squares and looks for O4 coming up the gut to the ball

- Next, he looks to O5 back on the ball-side low post

- Next, he looks to O2 if the wing defender *sags to cover the post*

- If the whole zone shifts, he can go back to O3

02

- Spots up and looks for a skip pass from O5

- Stays out of line and looks for a pass from O1 if the defense sags on the post

03

- Dribbles out of the corner and then pivots and passes to O5 in the short corner

- Occupies his man until O5 can get a look at O4 slicing down the key, or skips the ball

- Readies himself for a jumper if O1 or O2 skips the ball back to him

04

- Dives quickly from the high post as soon as O5 catches the ball in the short corner

- If he catches the ball on the slice cut, he powers it up

- If the ball gets passed from O5 to either O1 or O2, he follows it back to the high post

- Presents a big target in the high post, looking to catch and go through the four high post options

05

- Steps to the short corner from the low post and receives the pass from O3

- Immediately looks for O4 slicing from the high post

- Skips the ball across to either O1 or O2 and follows the pass across the key to the low post, angling up to give the passer a better angle

- Looks to catch and score from the low post

E. HIGH POST AWAY

Diagram 91

01
- Passes to 03 and V-cuts away and then comes back to the ball for a reversal

- Feeds 04 in the high post on the opposite side of the *court*

- Relocates on the far side of the shoot

02
- Gets out of line with the defense

- Looks to receive a pass and shoot

03
- Receives the pass from 01, squares to the basket and returns the ball to 01

- Gets out of line with the defense

- Looks to receive a pass from the high post and shoot

04
- Catches the ball from 01 in the high post

- Back pivots so he can see the whole floor and then goes through his sequence of options:

  —first look to his buddy in the low post

  —second look to the wing man opposite

—third look to the point on the far side of the shoot

—fourth look to the same-side wing

O5

- Stays on the opposite side of the high post man

- Ducks in hard when the ball gets passed to the high post man

- Catches and scores on the low block

- Occupies the defense by keeping a body on the defenders if he does not catch the ball

F. DRIBBLE OVERLOAD

We use this set if we want to make their guards, rather than their forwards, cover the wing area. Again, this set is used if we want to isolate a specific player because of his lack of defensive skills or his foul trouble.

Diagram 92

O1

- Dribbles the ball to the wing area and pushes O2 to the corner

- Looks to feed O2 in the corner for the jump shot or for a better angle to feed the post

- Looks to feed O5 in the low post

- Looks to reverse the ball through O4 in the high post, or O3 at the point

02
- Fades to the corner and readies himself to catch and shoot

- Looks to feed 05 in the low post

- Could hit 04 for the reversal or the high-low feed

- Skips to 03 at the far side of the shoot

03
- Fills the point as 01 vacates and sets up for reversal

04
- Stays in the high post area, square to the ball

- Looks to shoot or for a high-low feed or reversal

05
- Posts hard in the low post

- Looks to pin and seal if the ball is reversed

- Always looks for the high-low game with his buddy in the high post

G. BUDDIES

This maneuver is run for our post players. It is intended to combat people who try to front us in the low post area.

Diagram 93

01
- Passes the ball to 02 and relocates

- Receives the return pass and reverses the ball to 03 on the wing

02
- Receives the initial entry pass and returns the ball to 01 for a reversal

- Next, he cuts through to the ball-side corner to create a box

03
- Receives the ball from 01 on the ball-side wing and reads that 05 is being fronted

- Either passes the ball to 02 in the corner or *hits 04 on a lob* after 05 screens the low post defender who is fronting him

04
- Is on the ball-side high post, asking for the ball

- Follows the ball across the high post as it is reversed

- As soon as he sees that 05 is being fronted, he yells "buddies" and cuts to the basket, looking for the lob from either 02 or 03

05
- Stays in the low post on either side of the floor

- Posts or flashes to the low post ball-side as the ball is being reversed and 02 goes to the corner

- If 05 is fronted, he yells "buddies" and steps up to screen the man fronting him to open the area behind him for 04 to cut and receive the lob

H. POP

Diagram 94

Pop is the zone action that we use most of the time, because it is difficult to match up with for any type of zone. This offense was used against our matchup years ago, and we found it very difficult to defend. We have taken the action and modified it to suit our personnel every year.

01
- Dribbles the ball to the wing and looks for three post people to make their cuts

- *First, he looks for* 03 stepping out to the short corner

- Second, he looks for 05 diving from the high post to the low post

- Third, he looks for 04 filling in the high post

- If the post people are covered, he can skip the ball to 02

- After passing, he spots up out of line

02
- Goes away to the opposite wing and gets out of line with the defense

- Prepares for the pass and shot from 01 (skip), 03 (short corner), 04 (high post)

03
- Pops out to the short corner, looking for a pass and shot

- Can feed 05 slicing from the high post or 04 flashing to the high post

- Can skip the ball with a diagonal pass to 02

04
- Flashes to the ball side and stays under the top line of the zone

- Keeps his shoulders square and looks to catch and shoot or feed high-low

- Can also catch and reverse the ball to 02

05
- Slices from the high post to the low post, looking for the ball

- Keeps his shoulders square to the player with the ball at all times

- Works to catch the ball, but if he doesn't, he must occupy the defenders in the post

POP—CONT.

The pop series is also effective against any type of half-court trap because you are constantly bringing people to the ball in the middle of the floor.

What follows is a continuation of the pop series. Instead of describing the movement by position, I will describe the movement by spots.

Diagram 95

BALL-SIDE GUARD:

- Stays out of line with the defense

- If he catches the ball, he looks to feed either the short corner, the low post or the high post

- Can skip the ball back to the other guard

- If the ball is skipped back to him, he must always be ready to shoot

OFFSIDE GUARD:

- Stays out of line with the defense and prepares to shoot if the ball is skipped to him

SHORT CORNER:

- Always flashes into the high post and tries to stay under the guards so he is able to attack the bottom of the zone two-on-one

- Catches the ball at the high post and goes through his four high post options

LOW POST MAN:

- Drags across the lane, looking for the ball, and continues on to the short corner

HIGH POST MAN:

- Goes from high to low on the opposite side of the floor

- Looks for the ball the whole time he is making his diagonal cut to the post

Remember, the movement is as follows:

 —Low post drags across to the short corner

 —High post moves to the low block opposite

 —Short corner moves to the high post

CONCLUSION

Although we have tried other ideas and offenses for years, we always keep coming back to the same concepts described in this book. With small adjustments and the addition of some quick hitters that suit our personnel each year, what has been discussed here is the core of our zone offense. These concepts seem to have passed the ultimate test—the test of time.

I would like to thank my father, my staff and all the others who have worked with me in the past for their input and continual refinement of what we do. Their expertise has been invaluable.

I hope this book has helped you. More important, I hope it has helped to improve this great game we all love so much. Best of luck, and let's all keep working in every way to make this game even better.

Bob Huggins is a proven success as a program-builder, recruiter, game strategist and motivator. He has demonstrated this in a myriad of ways since joining the University of Cincinnati in 1989.

Inheriting a team that was short on numbers, Huggins inspired his initial team to a post season tournament and has done so every year since. Coach Huggins has compiled an impressive 247-82 record in his first 10 years at Cincinnati, making him the winningest coach in U. C. history.

For his efforts, Coach Huggins has been awarded many coaching honors, including the Ray Meyer Award as the Conference USA Coach of the Year in 1997 and 1998. He was also Basketball Times' selection for national coach of the year in 1997–'98, and was Playboy magazine's national coach of the year in 1992-'93.

Huggins began his coaching career as a graduate assistant at his alma mater, The University of West Virginia, in 1997. Subsequent coaching stints have included Ohio State (1978–'80), Walsh College (1980–'83), Central Florida (1983), and the University of Akron (1984–'89).

Born in Morgantown, W. Va., Huggins grew up in Gnadenhutten, Ohio where he played high school basketball for his father, Charles Huggins, at Gnadenhutten Indian Valley South. Bob and his wife, June, have two daughters, Jenna and Jacqueline.